AT THE EDGE OF NIGHT
AU BORD DE LA NUIT

Anise Koltz
AT THE EDGE OF NIGHT
AU BORD DE LA NUIT

Translated by
Anne-Marie Glasheen

Introduced by Caroline Price

2009

Published by Arc Publications,
Nanholme Mill, Shaw Wood Road
Todmorden OL14 6DA, UK

Original poems copyright © Anise Koltz 2009
Translation copyright © Anne-Marie Glasheen 2009
Introduction copyright © Caroline Price 2009

Design by Tony Ward
Printed by the MPG Books Group in the UK

978 1904614 56 2 (pbk)
978 1906570 03 3 (hbk)

ACKNOWLEDGEMENTS

The poems in this book have been selected from four collections by Anise Koltz, all published with the aid of the Fonds Culturel National, Luxembourg, as follows: *Le cri de l'épervier* (The Call of the Sparrow-hawk), Editions PHI, Luxembourg, 2000; *Le porteur d'ombre* (Shadow-bearer), Editions PHI, Luxembourg, 2001; *L'avaleur de feu* (Fire-eater), Editions PHI, Luxembourg, 2003; and *Béni soit le serpent* (Blessed be the Serpent), Editions PHI, Luxembourg, 2004.

Cover photograph: © Anne-Marie Glasheen

This book is in copyright. Subject to statutory exception and to provision of relevant collective licensing agreements, no reproduction of any part of this book may take place without the written permission of Arc Publications.

The publishers acknowledge financial assistance
from ACE Yorkshire

Arc Publications 'Visible Poets' series
Editor: Jean Boase-Beier

for Jacqui

Poetry must have something in it that is
barbaric, vast and wild.

Denis Diderot, 1713-1784

CONTENTS

Series Editor's Note / 13
Translator's Preface / 15
Introduction / 22

from / de
THE CALL OF THE SPARROW-HAWK / LE CRI DE L'ÉPERVIER

32 / Le cri de l'épervier •	The Call of the Sparrow-hawk / 33
32 / Le paysage immobile •	The Rigid Landscape / 33
34 / Lumière glaciale •	Icy Light / 35
34 / Pansements •	Dressings / 35
36 / Commune origine •	Common Origin / 37
36 / Le corbeau •	The Crow / 37
38 / Sommeil blanc •	Fretful Sleep / 39
38 / Mille enclumes •	A Thousand Anvils / 39
40 / Bête de nuit •	Night Animal / 41
40 / Outils de pierre •	Stone Tools / 41
42 / Voyante •	Clairvoyant / 43
42 / Le poète •	The Poet / 43
44 / La moitié •	Half / 45
44 / La terre •	The Earth / 45
46 / La langue de nos pères •	Our Fathers' Tongue / 47
46 / Qui écrit ? •	Who writes? / 47
48 / A ma mère •	To My Mother / 49
48 / Automne •	Autumn / 49
50 / A ma mère •	To My Mother / 51
50 / Sans fin •	Endless / 51
52 / La lune •	The Moon / 53
52 / Distances •	Distances / 53
54 / L'homme ne me couvre plus •	The Man No Longer covers Me / 55
54 / Ne parle plus •	Stop talking / 55
56 / Les crimes de ce siècle •	This Century's Crimes / 57
56 / Trahison •	Betrayal / 57

from / de
Shadow-bearer / Le porteur d'ombre

60 / Prologue	Prologue / 61
60 / "J'avance sans filet…"	"I advance without a net…" / 61
62 / Désert	Desert / 63
64 / "Le chemin monte…"	"The path leads up…" / 65
66 / "Je dédie ce poème…"	"I dedicate this poem…" / 67
66 / "La maison de mon père…"	"My father's house…" / 67
68 / "La guerre a éclaté…"	"War has broken out…" / 69
68 / "Dans les vitrines des magasins…"	"In shop windows…" / 69
70 / "Courez dit-il…"	"Run he said…" / 71
70 / "Sur une mappe monde…"	"On a map of the world…" / 71
72 / "Dans le fleuve…"	"In the river…" / 73
72 / "Même si j'habite…"	"Though I live…" / 73
74 / "Océan je suis les humeurs…"	"Ocean I follow the moods…" / 75
74 / "Mon père m'a transmis…"	"My father handed me…" / 75
76 / "Mon frère plongeur sous-marin…"	"My deep-sea diving brother…" / 77
76 / Sable	Sand / 77
78 / Ciel	Sky / 79
78 / Vent	Wind / 79
80 / "J'ai peur du livre…"	"I'm afraid of the book…" / 81
80 / "Dans ce monde…"	"In this world…" / 81
82 / "Tu voudrais connaître…"	"You would know…" / 83
82 / "Mes poèmes…"	"My poems…" / 83
84 / "Je me débats…"	"I struggle…" / 85
84 / Chaleur	Heat / 85
86 / Froid	Cold / 87
86 / Entre chien et loup	At Dusk: Between Dog and Wolf / 87

from
Fire-eater / L'avaleur de feu

I

90 / "Il est parti…" • "He left…" / 91
92 / "Il n'y a pas de route…" • "There is no road…" / 93
92 / "Tu es celui…" • "You are the one…" / 93
94 / "Lorsque mon amour…" • "When my love…" / 95

II

94 / "Depuis toujours…" • "All my life…" / 95
96 / "Ma mémoire est lourde…" • "My memory is heavy…" / 97
96 / "La lune a empoisonné mes livres…" • "The moon has poisoned my books…" / 97
98 / "Je me décline…" • "I fade…" / 99

III

98 / "Dans les abattoirs de l'église…" • "In the abattoirs of the church…" / 99
100 / "Je cherche un baptistère…" • "I'm searching for a baptistery…" / 101
100 / "Aucune de nos complaintes…" • "None of our laments…" / 101
102 / "L'ange déchu…" • "The fallen angel…" / 103
102 / "Le septième jour…" • "On the seventh day…" / 103

IV

104 / "A mon réveil…" • "When I wake up…" / 105
104 / "Tiré par des chiens…" • "Drawn by dogs…" / 105
106 / "La nuit…" • "At night…" / 107
106 / "Maintenant que je suis habituée…" • "Now I am grown used… / 107
108 / "Je partirai…" • "I shall leave…" / 109
108 / "Chaque nuit…" • "Every night…" / 109

V

110 / "Mon absence…" • "My absence…" / 111
110 / "Après le passage…" • "After the passing…" / 111

112 / "Combien de fois…" • "How many times…" / 113

VI

112 / "A ma naissance…" • "At my birth…" / 113
114 / "L'enfant dévore…" • "The child devours…" / 115
114 / "Je suis l'erreur fatale…" • "I am my father's fatal error…" / 115
116 / "Il ne faut pas chercher…" • "Do not seek…" / 117

from
BLESSED BE THE SERPENT / BÉNI SOIT LE SERPENT

I

120 / "Ne me retiens pas…" • "Don't hold me back…" / 121
122 / "Ma mère…" • "My mother…" / 123
122 / "J'ai eu des centaines de mères…" • "I had hundreds of mothers…" / 123
124 / "Mes pieds sans racines…" • "My rootless feet…" / 125
124 / "Etranger je demeure…" • "Foreigner I remain…" / 125
126 / "Sous ma peau…" • "Under my skin…" / 127
128 / "Sur le corps de ma mère…" • "On my mother's body…" / 129
128 / "Où que j'aille…" • "Wherever I go…" / 129

II

130 / Il Satiro danzante • Il Satiro danzante / 131
132 / "Pendant la nuit…" • "During the night…" / 133

III

132 / "La lune vient se reposer…" • "The moon comes and settles…" / 133
134 / "L'immensité de la mer…" • "The vastness of the sea…" / 135
134 / "Le soleil tend des filets…" • "The sun sets a trap…" / 135

IV

136 / "Mes mots sont habitués à la guerre…" • "My words are grown used to war…" / 137

136 / "Il n'y a pas d'espoir…" • "There is no hope…" / 137
138 / "La vie dépend…" • "Life depends…" / 139
138 / "Par l'écriture…" • "Through writing…" / 139
140 / "L'écriture…" • "Writing…" / 141
140 / "Mon poème…" • "My poem…" / 141
142 / "Lorsque les paroles…" • "When words…" / 143

V

142 / "Depuis 76 ans…" • "For 76 years…" / 143
144 / "Je déracine des étoiles…" • "I uproot stars…" / 145

VI

144 / "Tes pas ont inventé…" • "Yours steps invented…" / 145
146 / "Nous parlons des langues différentes…" • "We speak different languages…" / 147

VII

146 / "Béni soit le serpent…" • "Blessed be the serpent…" / 147
148 / "Apres avoir verrouillé…" • "Having bolted up…" / 149

Biographical Notes / 151

SERIES EDITOR'S NOTE

There is a prevailing view of translated poetry, especially in England, which maintains that it should read as though it had originally been written in English. The books in the 'Visible Poets' series aim to challenge that view. They assume that the reader of poetry is by definition someone who wants to experience the strange, the unusual, the new, the foreign, someone who delights in the stretching and distortion of language which makes any poetry, translated or not, alive and distinctive. The translators of the poets in this series aim not to hide but to reveal the original, to make it visible and, in so doing, to render visible the translator's task too. The reader is invited not only to experience the unique fusion of the creative talents of poet and translator embodied in the English poems in these collections, but also to speculate on the processes of their creation and so to gain a deeper understanding and enjoyment of both original and translated poems.

Jean Boase-Beier

TRANSLATOR'S PREFACE

*'My poems are pilgrims that take off their shoes before all speech.
Spoken with too much confidence, the latter loses its power.'*
                                                        Anise Koltz

I no longer remember when I first discovered the poetry of Anise Koltz – it might sound clichéd but I feel as though I have always known it. The sparseness and brevity of the poems and the impact that these produce; the recurring themes – the nature of writing, the parent-child relationship, the place of religion in a less than perfect world, the loss of the husband, issues of identity, the passing of time and with it life, death and the hereafter – are those that concern me also. And as each collection dropped through my letterbox, I was each time compelled to start translating it.

A philosophical poet, her poetic visions are both deeply personal and deeply universal. And whilst there is optimism, even joy, in her work, there is also a sense of sadness, a sense of disappointment. Her work often pulses with violence and rage – rage against her parents, herself, life, the world and God. Her skill as a wordsmith and the succinctness of her poems combine to give us glimpses of her personal pain and her more universal anger.

The force of her message – the thought – is more important to her than poetic features such as rhythm or rhyme, and yet her poems have a song-like quality to them, particularly when they seem to cry out from the void to reverberate in the world. This 'void', however, is not always a negative space – it is the '…one crater / studded with pebbles' in which the poet can draw on the sustenance of words.

'Trauma turned me to writing in German, trauma then turned me to writing in French', Anise Koltz explained in an interview in 2002. She had been writing in German for twenty years, but the death of her husband who had never fully recovered from his time as a prisoner of the Nazis, made it impossible for her to continue to do so. And it was only after a long period of silence that she began to write again, and then almost exclusively in French.

Though obviously fluent in French, it is not Koltz's first language – to her French was an 'acquired' language. True Luxembourgers are brought up speaking Luxembourgish (long regarded as a German dialect but now recognised as a minority language), the language that is the heart and soul of their identity. Education takes place primarily in German and then also in French. Luxembourgish writers are invariably multilingual. Koltz acknowledges that she has Germanic rather than French sensibilities. In the same 2002 interview, she goes on to state that there is a world of difference between German and French, and that when a Germanic sensibility is *transfused* into a Latin language, something almost physical takes place – the *transfusion* produces a kind of *spark*. Moreover the people of Luxembourg are a very mixed people, and whilst they are not German as such, they have a lot of German blood in them. So, not only are their sensibilities different from their French and Belgian neighbours, but their use of the French language is different from that of those who speak it on a daily basis – much like the English spoken in Ireland is different from that spoken in England. Their great advantage is that they are able to follow the flow of two great cultures – French and German – in the original language rather than in translation.

Koltz grew up in the post-war period when the intellectual atmosphere in Luxembourg, as elsewhere in Europe, was saturated in existential philosophy. Such concepts as 'ennui', the liberty of the individual, the 'void' of being, the hostility of the 'other', the destructiveness of this other's 'gaze', the impossibility of any true contact with the consciousness of the 'other', the meaninglessness of man's presence on earth, were issues that were hotly debated. There is an existential undercurrent to Koltz's œuvre. But despite having introduced her collection *Chants de refus* with a quote from Samuel

Beckett – 'Silence is our mother tongue' – she is a poet who is far from silent.

Selecting the poems was no easy task; I decided to concentrate on the four collections I had, all published in this new millennium. And unable to include all the poems, I picked around the same number from each of the collections, and chose poems from each part of each sequence. From a translator's point of view, there were no major challenges and I had very few queries as to meaning, and any ambiguities were quickly resolved. When reviewing the manuscript, I tightened up the language by dropping words and sometimes substituted, for the sake of succinctness, a one- or two-syllable word where I had originally used a longer one to ensure the poems retained their almost aphoristic form.

All but the last collection of the four represented here, *Béni soit le serpent* (Blessed be the Serpent), contain photographs – like visual echoes of her own poetic visions – taken by the author of places she has visited. In all four collections, the lines of the poems are short, sometimes no more than a word or two; the verses too are brief. The sometimes-enigmatic language is pared down to its barest essentials. Each poem – though a part of a sequence, and each sequence a part of the whole – stands alone. The brevity of the poems and the simplicity of the language make her images all the more powerful. And it is no palette knife that she uses to build her poems, but delicate brushstrokes.

> Sometimes I embark on a subject then it blurs and something else comes to the surface dictated from inside and I finish up with something different. I begin one way and end up another. It often happens. Subjects often preoccupy me.

In *Le cri de l'épervier* (The Call of the Sparrow-hawk), each of Anise Koltz's poems seems born of the conflict between a life that pulses, quivers and falters and a hostile universe. But in the face of this hostility the poet is defiant.

> God is no longer my master
> my sleep will be fretful
> foamy like the ocean (p. 39)

The recurrent themes are there from the start: her fixation with death, her anger towards God, her take on writing, the husband who is no longer there, the loathing of the mother. 'I am never done / with my mother' she declares, 'Dying / she admitted / that she was born / with but half a heart.' (p. 45)

In *Le porteur d'ombre* (Shadow-bearer), Anise Koltz tells us right at the start that 'Life is no long quiet river'. She invites us to take a good look at the world and to reflect upon what we see. This is done either directly through actual references and / or indirectly through images taken from our immediate environment and daily lives.

> War has broken out
> television
> delivers to our homes
> the day's dead and injured
> with a cheese and pasta
> stuffing
>
> Sometimes someone leaves
> the table to spit out
> non-existent fish-bones (p. 69)

Koltz draws our attention to the apocalyptic times in which we live and communicates her disgust and revolt at the state of the world. Her anger is evident. But can words, can poetry save the world? In the Prologue, she warns us: 'each of my poems / buries your dead'. What follows is 'desert', and what follows is also a look at her own life.

The section headings that create the desert environment are very elemental: 'desert' and 'sand' – earth, 'sky' and 'wind' – air, 'heat' – fire, and 'cold' – water; whilst the last section 'at dusk' is temporal. The headings are to some extent impressionistic and therefore well suited to her style and language. In the desert at dusk (twixt day and night, heat and cold, or twixt 'dog and wolf' to translate the French expression for 'at dusk' literally) man is at his most vulnerable.

The whole collection is permeated with a sense of finitude, for are we not all Shadow-bearers? Are we not all not only condemned to die, but, paradoxically, also condemned to eternity. The collection ends with the words: 'We are immortal / as long as we live'.

In *L'Avaleur de feu* (Fire-eater), there is a return to the self, to the poet feeling compelled to look at past and future ordeals. Divided into seven sections, the first is filled with sorrow at the memory of her husband: 'Along with my hair / my sadness continues / to grow'. (p. 91)

Again we find the threat of the void, the nature of writing, the blank page that stalks her like a predator: 'the empty pages / watch me and hound me / like wolves'. (p. 97) The very act of writing is an act of violence. And she is as much the torturer as the victim – like so many poets her sense of exile is great.

Revisiting the past and journeying through herself, the poet examines not only her life and the world but also her relationship with God.

> None of our laments
> will be heard
>
> God is deaf and dumb
> No one has taught us
> sign language   (p. 101)

In the final section she returns to her greatest anger, her anger towards her parents – the source of the original wound:

> Do not seek
> the father in the father
> nor the mother
> in the mother
>
> they invented me
> sculpting me
> with an axe. (p. 117)

Béni soit le serpent (Blessed be the Serpent) is the most recent of these collections and probably where, at the age of 76, she is the most conscious of drawing closer to the moment when she will cease to be. But there are still things to do, journeys to make, before her time runs out. There is a new urgency in the jerkiness of the rhythm. The themes are the same, but there is no sense that she is repeating herself; on the contrary, whilst her honesty and directness remain uncompromised, there is a freshness to her approach.

> Wherever I go
> I carry my corpse
> with me
>
> Each night
> I sacrifice it
> to the setting sun
>
> Together we daub the sky
> with blood. (p. 129)

The poet still, she does not mince her words; she is once again catapulting her barbed words into our lives. 'When words / no longer inhabit / my mouth // I shall fill it / with stones' (p. 143) – words that speak of suffering, words that describe the experience that is that long uninterrupted journey – life. We travel with her from her birth (which she regrets) to her death (which is never far from her thoughts) and through her inner journeys (which are inseparable from those she has undertaken on the planet).

> The vastness of the sea
> passes through me
>
> It overflows
> from my shoes (p. 135)

Anise Koltz's poetry has a lyricism, a purity and immediacy, that makes her voice unique. In my view she is Luxembourg's greatest living poet and her poetry is among Europe's finest. Hers is a poetic voice imbued with much needed wisdom at the start of a new millennium that has seen no end to aggression and self-interest; hers is a soft but unwavering voice that advocates generosity of spirit, and which deserves to be more widely heard. Koltz's poetry has won many prizes but in Paris, in June 1998, she was awarded the prestigious Prix Apollinaire for her collection *Le mur du son*.

It is unfortunate that the literature of Luxembourg is underrepresented in the English-speaking world. Two Luxembourg poets Liliane Welsh (now living and working in Canada) and Pierre Joris (living and working in the USA) have been widely published, but both of them write in English. John F. Deane's translation of Anise Koltz, *At the Devil's Banquets* (The Dedalus Press, Dublin, 1998) and my translation of Jean Portante's *Point / Erasing* (The Dedalus Press, Dublin, 2003) are the first and only two collections by any poet from Luxembourg to be translated into English. There are other poets waiting to be discovered.

Anne-Marie Glasheen

INTRODUCTION

I first read Anise Koltz's work in *At the Devil's Banquets*, a selection from three of her previous collections made and translated by John F. Deane for the Dedalus Press in 1998 and, until this point, the only poetry of hers to be published in English translation. She is introduced on the book's cover as "Luxembourg's best-known poet", but despite that, and her long literary career – she is now in her late seventies and has published more or less continuously over the past forty years – she is little known in the English-speaking literary world. This further selection of her work is therefore very much to be welcomed.

Anise Koltz was born in Luxembourg in 1928, at a time when Luxembourg literature was still fighting to establish its own identity, not just in relation to the wider world, but within its own borders. This struggle was due in part to the particular linguistic environment: in a country where Letzebürgesch, French and German are spoken and written equally, no single literature has been able to develop, but rather a three-stranded one, reflecting different currents in Romance and Germanic cultures at different times, into which the Luxembourg writer has been free to dip at choice.

Even within the country, literature has had to struggle to be recognised as a significant medium. A true national identity did not evolve until Luxembourg's borders and independence were confirmed in the mid-nineteenth century, and poetry did not really start to develop until the early decades of the twentieth century. Even then, the pace of industrial advance, the country's geographical position and two world wars made it hard for writers from the Grand Duchy to find a voice of their own. There was a tendency to withdraw, to draw on and idealize their immediate surroundings rather than look to the outside world for inspiration.

However, as the century progressed, things began to change. Little by little, new writers began to emerge, more ambitious and critical and keen to move away from the rather old-fashioned, insular conservatism of their predecessors. As a literary confidence developed, multilingualism, previously viewed as a hindrance, came to be seen as an asset. Publishing houses were founded, raising the profile of writers in the country and abroad. Today Luxembourg literature is in a very healthy state, and work in all three languages has flourished, with French frequently seeming to be the preferred language for poetry.

Anise Koltz published her first collection of poetry in 1959 when she was thirty-one, and three years later she initiated her lifelong commitment to Luxembourg literature when she founded the Journées de Montdorf, a festival designed to promote ties between Luxembourg authors and writers from abroad and which was to have a profound effect on the development of poetry within the country. The same year, she was awarded the Prix du Gouvernment luxembourgeois, the first of many prizes that have marked her career. For the first two decades of her writing life she wrote in German, but after her husband's death in 1971 (he was, we are told in brief biographical notes, 'a late victim of the Nazi occupation'), she switched to writing poetry in French and has done so ever since. Interestingly, the younger Luxembourg poet Jean Portante, who has worked closely with Anise Koltz for many years, notes that her French is very German-like, and suggests that this is what gives her work some of its artistic power.

And artistic power it certainly has. This is poetry unlike any I have come across before. It feels utterly European, and at the same time it is completely accessible. It speaks to the reader directly, jumping cultural barriers. It is poetry which is knife-sharp, clear, and dazzling.

The four collections from which this selection has been taken were published between 2000 and 2004, products of an extremely prolific seventh decade. In them, Anise Koltz returns again and again to the themes which have always preoccupied her, but with increasing insistence and precision; as she feels time running out, so it becomes more and more urgent to find words – and the *right* words – to describe the human condition, and the states of the human mind as it confronts the void.

> In this world
> stripped of meaning
> language is our last refuge
>
> It is what bids our present
> exist   (p. 81)

The poems fall into natural groups and are arranged in an inherently dramatic sequence within each collection, moving through the human to the metaphysical questions of eternity and the hereafter. Each collection has its particular emphasis: defiance is present from the outset in *Le cri de l'épervier* (The Call of the Sparrow-hawk); *Le porteur d'ombre* (Shadow-bearer), dedicated to her husband and her granddaughter, is bleaker, and full of anger. *L'avaleur de feu* (Fire-eater) has a sadder, more elegiac tone, and the poems are more personal, whereas *Béni soit le serpent* (Blessed be the Serpent) hovers on the very border between existence and non-existence. But the overarching feeling, taking the poems as a whole, is that we are accompanying the writer on a long, unbroken journey, towards silence, towards death – a writer who never stops asking questions, who is determined to use words until her breath runs out, even as she becomes increasingly aware of their inadequacy.

> Through writing
> I penetrate
> the impossible
>
> Beneath the grazes of the letters
> the ink that flows is my blood   (p. 139)

The juxtaposition of opposites underlies all her poetry, and this contributes to its great tension – a tension which is enhanced by the absolute economy of her writing. This is writing that has been pared down to its essentials; there is not a word more than necessary. The poems are short – often extremely so. The lines are short, and the stanzas clearly separated. Other than the occasional dash or question mark, there is no punctuation, the line breaks conveying all the sense that is necessary. Her language is strong, direct and simple; she is never tempted to embellish what she is saying with rhyme or rich imagery. There is no self-indulgence here. The images she uses are recognisable, concrete, rooted in the world we are all familiar with. She makes her purpose quite clear to the reader:

Life is no long quiet river
but a bloodbath

Yet you ask me for
poetry decorated with flowers
with little birds

I'm sorry Ladies and Gentlemen
each of my poems
buries your dead (p. 61)

What comes across, in poetry this concise, is the meticulous care with which each word has been chosen. Just as Anise Koltz wants in her work to go straight to the heart of human existence, so she aims to find a language that is as pure as it is possible to be. The result is a poetry which feels intensely sharp and "right". Her poems have the precision of aphorisms; tiny as they are, they open onto enormous vistas. They resonate in the mind; they force us to think. Even if we don't share her opinions, we feel instinctively that we can relate to the "truth" of what she is saying. She makes us continually aware of paradoxes – of the power of words, and of their frailty, as in this poem dedicated to her husband:

> My breath utters
> the beloved's name
> it is but a little mist
> a few letters
> of the alphabet   (p. 91)

Although her poems are so short, they bristle with pent-up anger – at the human condition:

> Every mealtime
> our table becomes
> a battleground
>
> An entire bestiary disappears
> from our plates
> sky and earth
> pass through our stomachs   (p. 63)

and at a God that can let this happen:

> each day
> the bible must be rewritten
> by the icy light
> of the world   (p. 35)

And time and again she returns to the struggle we all have to break free of our parents. The ambiguity of her relationship with her mother is ruthlessly portrayed:

> I carried her
> on my shoulders
>
> Beneath this invisible burden
> I collapsed   (p. 129)

As she fights to find her own identity, she constantly questions the preconceptions and secure faith of her Catholic background. She has voluntarily cast herself out:

> I am Eve
> banished from paradise
> and become clairvoyant   (p. 43)

and feels privileged to be so:

> Blessed be the serpent
> who taught me disobedience   (p. 147)

because this is the only way to find knowledge; even if it means being – as poets surely are – in permanent exile:

> Pursue your wandering
> in this rigid landscape
> he who stops
> is lost   (p. 33)

The night is a recurringly potent place; it is seen as a rehearsal for death, and, partly because of that, a place where the truth can be most closely arrived at:

> During the night
> I howl like a wolf
>
> ...
>
> When I wake
> I look in the mirror
> and see a familiar Anise Koltz
> with an innocent air –
>
> But with my chops covered in fresh blood   (p. 133)

As she moves nearer to the void, the more she prepares herself:

> I shall leave
> shoeless
> aimless
>
> Distraught
> my guardian angel
> will discard the mounting
> for his wings   (p. 109)

Her poetry teeters almost unbearably painfully, by the end, between the acknowledgement of the smallness of human life:

> My absence
> begun long ago
> before my departure
> stretches
> beyond my return (p. 111)

and the determination not to give in:

> A night
> beyond night
> awaits us
> ...
>
> We are immortal
> as long as we live (p. 87)

These are poems which resonate far beyond their size; which light up like flares and stay in the mind and memory. They are stark, they can be bleak, but their purity and lucidness invests them with a rare and extraordinary beauty. Easy to empathize with these words in a recent review (A. Levesque, 2005):

> The poems of Anise Koltz are poems to share, to write like graffiti upon misfortune's many surfaces. And hope and something of beauty will lodge there to be found by those who go looking for small pleasures.

Caroline Price

AT THE EDGE OF NIGHT
AU BORD DE LA NUIT

from
THE CALL OF THE SPARROW-HAWK
LE CRI DE L'ÉPERVIER

LE CRI DE L'ÉPERVIER

Lorsque la mort
me traverse
j'arrache son cri
à l'épervier
et l'intègre
à mon vocabulaire

LE PAYSAGE IMMOBILE

En ce jour transparent
la lumière couve les pierres

Si tu touches la terre
elle s'émiette

La parole éclate de chaleur

Continue ton errance
dans ce paysage immobile
celui qui s'arrête
est perdu

THE CALL OF THE SPARROW-HAWK

When death
passes through me
I seize his call
from the sparrow-hawk
and integrate it
into my vocabulary

THE RIGID LANDSCAPE

On this transparent day
light sits on the stones

If you touch the earth
it crumbles

Speech explodes with heat

Pursue your wandering
in this rigid landscape
he who stops
is lost

LUMIÈRE GLACIALE

Chaque jour
notre destin chancèle
chaque jour
la bible est à réécrire
sous la lumière glaciale
du monde

PANSEMENTS

Sous un soleil brûlant
qui arrache les peaux
ton corps fouille le mien
cherchant des pansements
pour tes blessures

ICY LIGHT

Each day
our destiny reels
each day
the bible must be rewritten
by the icy light
of the world

DRESSINGS

Beneath a burning sun
that tears off skins
your body rifles mine
in search of dressings
for your wounds

COMMUNE ORIGINE

Chaque cours d'eau
connaît par cœur
le chemin vers la mer

Ainsi que mon sang
qui revendique
une commune origine

Même mes poèmes
sont peuplés
de monstres marins
engloutissant les dieux
qui marchent sur les flots

LE CORBEAU

Sous ma chemise
je porte la mort
tel un corbeau
apprenti de la parole

Il est seul à comprendre
le langage enragé de mon cœur

COMMON ORIGIN

Every watercourse
knows by heart
the way to the sea

Like my blood
which proclaims
a common origin

Even my poems
are peopled
with sea monsters
swallowing up the gods
who walk on the billows

THE CROW

Inside my shirt
I carry death
like a crow
apprentice to speech

Only he understands
the rabid language of my heart

SOMMEIL BLANC

J'ai détruit le baptistère de l'église
que mon nom soit banni à jamais

Dieu n'est plus mon maître
mon sommeil sera blanc
écumeux comme l'océan

MILLE ENCLUMES

L'avenir n'est plus à moi –
J'ai vendu mon âme au diable

Dans mon sang résonnent
mille enclumes
sans aucun forgeron

FRETFUL SLEEP

I destroyed the baptistery
so that my name would be forever banished

God is no longer my master
my sleep will be fretful
foamy like the ocean

A THOUSAND ANVILS

The future is no longer mine –
I sold my soul to the devil

In my blood resound
a thousand anvils
without a single blacksmith

BÊTE DE NUIT

Tu bois la pluie
dans ma bouche

Ton souffle sauvage
balaie ma peau

Toute ta nature
se déchaîne contre moi

Je suis une bête de nuit
qui rôde dans tes pâturages

OUTILS DE PIERRE

Je pénètre dans ta mémoire
lorsque tu t'assoupis

Je couche mon nom
dans le tien

Tandis que tes souvenirs s'estompent
 je t'entraîne vers la caverne préhistorique
que j'habite
avec mes outils de pierre
dont je fais jaillir le feu

NIGHT ANIMAL

You drink the rain
in my mouth

Your feral breath
brushes my skin

Your whole nature
rages at me

I am a night animal
prowling in your pastures

STONE TOOLS

I enter your memory
when you doze off

I lay my name
in yours

As your memories fade
I lead you to the prehistoric cave
where I live
with my stone tools
that bring forth fire

VOYANTE

Je suis Eve
chassée du paradis
et devenue voyante

Je n'élève plus mes enfants
comme des larves

Dieu n'a pas besoin
de les délivrer du mal

Chaque arbre
est celui de la connaissance

LE POÈTE

Devant lui
la feuille blanche
étendue comme une plage
où les mots courent
brûlés par le large
sans cesse perturbés
par des secousses inattendues

Plusieurs personnes
peuvent mourir
dans un mot

CLAIRVOYANT

I am Eve
banished from paradise
and become clairvoyant

I no longer bring up my children
as though they were larvae

God has no need
to deliver them from evil

Each tree
is that of knowledge

THE POET

In front of him
the blank page
sprawling like a beach
where words run around
burnt by the open sea
constantly disrupted
by unexpected tremors

Several people
can die
in a word

LA MOITIÉ

Je n'en finis pas
avec ma mère

Mourante
elle m'a avoué
qu'elle n'était née
qu'avec la moitié de son cœur

LA TERRE

Quand tu marches
tu sens la terre
s'agripper
à tes semelles

Elle n'oublie pas de t'oublier

HALF

I am never done
with my mother

Dying
she admitted
that she was born
with but half a heart

THE EARTH

When you walk
you feel the earth
cling
to your soles

It doesn't forget to forget you

LA LANGUE DE NOS PÈRES

Notre langue maternelle
est celle de nos pères

Le verbe se raidit
sous la froideur de leur souffle

Tandis que nous
suspendons le temps
et leur linge
derrière la maison

QUI ÉCRIT ?

Toxicomane de la parole
je m'endors sous son poids

Est-ce moi qui écris le poème ?
est-ce le poème qui m'écrit ?

OUR FATHERS' TONGUE

Our mother tongue
is that of our fathers

The word stiffens
in the coldness of their breath

While we
suspend time
and their washing
behind the house

WHO WRITES?

Addict of speech
I fall asleep under its weight

Is it I that write the poem?
is it the poem that writes me?

A MA MÈRE

Tu m'as rempli la bouche
de mots
que je ne connaissais pas

A quoi ont-ils servi ?

La langue de jadis
n'est pas celle d'aujourd'hui

Et même ton sang
me marquant
à ma naissance
n'est pas resté le tien

AUTOMNE

Le vieux chêne –
ton père
gaspillant ses feuilles
pièces d'or
perdues au jeu

TO MY MOTHER

You filled my mouth
with words
I did not know

What use were they?

Yesterday's tongue
is not that of today

And even your blood
that marked me
at my birth
is no longer yours

AUTUMN

The old oak –
your father
wasting his leaves
gold coins
lost gambling

A MA MÈRE

Tu pèses toujours sur moi
telle une pierre tombale
partout
l'immobilité règne
le vent est à bout de souffle

J'ignore si c'est en moi
ou depuis d'autres lieux
que se soulève la mémoire
obscur marécage
d'où tu ressuscites
pour me ligoter
avec ton cordon ombilical

SANS FIN

Ton corps me longe
en fleuve

Ma peau est sans fin

Tu me traverses
m'ensemençant de pierres

TO MY MOTHER

You still weigh on me
like a tombstone
everywhere
stillness prevails
the wind is out of breath

I know not if it's in me
or from elsewhere
that memory is stirred
dark marsh
whence you rise from the dead
to tie me up
with your umbilical cord

ENDLESS

Your body runs alongside me
like a river

My skin is endless

Passing through me
you inseminate me with stones

LA LUNE

J'entre dans l'âme des défunts
continuant leur errance

La lune prise de vertige
s'assied dans les arbres
et crie avec les oiseaux de nuit

DISTANCES

Le monde dans lequel je vis
est un monde de miroirs

Ce que je réussis
ne m'appartient plus

Ce que je n'accomplis pas
se vitrifie

Je vous parle
à des distances
de plus en plus éloignées

THE MOON

I enter the souls of the dead
continuing their restless wanderings

The moon become dizzy
sits in the trees
and calls with the night birds

DISTANCES

The world wherein I live
is a world of mirrors

What I succeed in doing
no longer belongs to me

What I do not achieve
vitrifies

I speak to you
from ever increasing
distances

L'HOMME NE ME COUVRE PLUS

L'homme ne me couvre plus
je suis seule
sous cette peau
qui flétrit
sans me prévenir
de ma mort

Le pain bientôt
se mangera sans moi

NE PARLE PLUS

Faute de me comprendre
tu me traduis –

Ne parle plus
crache les paroles
soudons nos corps
arrêtons l'univers

THE MAN NO LONGER COVERS ME

The man no longer covers me
I am alone
inside this skin
that fades
without warning me
of my death

The bread soon
will be eaten without me

STOP TALKING

Unable to understand me
you translate me –

Stop talking
spit out the words
let's fuse our bodies
let's stop the universe

LES CRIMES DE CE SIÈCLE

La lune apparaît
crâne rasé
une femme nazie
d'après-guerre

Elle connaît les crimes
de ce siècle
ayant contribué
à les éclairer

La lune expie ses péchés
crâne rasé
une femme nazie
d'après-guerre

TRAHISON

Seuls comme la terre qui tourne
nous tournons dans l'espace

Anges mortels
avec des ailes fracassées
trahis par un Dieu
qui tue
qui tue
qui tue

THIS CENTURY'S CRIMES

The moon appears
head shaved
a post-war
nazi woman

She knows this century's
crimes
having played a part
in shedding light on them

The moon expiates her sins
head shaved
a post-war
nazi woman

BETRAYAL

Alone like the earth that turns
we turn in space

Mortal angels
with broken wings
betrayed by a God
who kills
who kills
who kills

from
SHADOW-BEARER
LE PORTEUR D'OMBRE

to the memory of René Koltz
who died in 1971
and to my granddaughter Béryl

PROLOGUE

La vie n'est pas un long fleuve tranquille
elle est un carnage

Et vous me demandez
une poésie ornée de fleurs
de petits oiseaux

Excusez-moi Mesdames Messieurs
chacun de mes poèmes
enterre vos morts

* * *

J'avance sans filet
d'une étoile à l'autre
glissant à travers les trous noirs
je saute de lunes en soleils

Je me balance aux bords
de la terre
déjà je ne lui appartiens plus

Parce que ce poème est un mensonge
il a le droit d'être beau

PROLOGUE

Life is no long quiet river
but a bloodbath

Yet you ask me for
poetry decorated with flowers
with little birds

I'm sorry Ladies and Gentlemen
each of my poems
buries your dead

* * *

I advance without a net
from one star to another
sliding through black holes
I leap from moons to suns

I rock at the edges
of the earth
already no longer belonging to it

Because this poem is a lie
it has the right to be beautiful

DÉSERT

A chaque repas
notre table devient
un champ de bataille

Tout un bestiaire disparaît
de nos assiettes
ciel et terre
traversent nos estomacs

Nous oublions
les signes précurseurs
de l'apocalypse
qui porte des gants blancs
pour nous servir

DESERT

Every mealtime
our table becomes
a battleground

An entire bestiary disappears
from our plates
sky and earth
pass through our stomachs

We forget
the signs that herald
the apocalypse
that wears white gloves
to serve us

* * *

Le chemin monte vers la maison
comme toujours
mais les portes s'ouvrent
moins facilement

La mère s'interroge
sur le sens de la guerre

Le père mange
il ne parle plus

L'instant traîne
devant le mur du jardin

Le vent pousse
une balançoire oubliée

* * *

The path leads up to the house
as it always has
but the doors open
less easily

The mother mulls over
the meaning of war

The father eats
he no longer speaks

The moment lingers
at the garden wall

The wind pushes
a forgotten swing

* * *

Je dédie ce poème
à mon incapacité
de saisir mon entourage
le plus proche

A ces moments
qui n'ont pas lieu
qui me laissent
hors de toute compréhension

Je le dédie aux mots justes
que jamais je ne saurai dire
pour dénoncer ce siècle
barbare et sans honte

* * *

La maison de mon père
asile de fous
enfermait la vaste histoire du monde
réduite à quelque tomes
dans une bibliothèque verrouillée

Je cognais en jurant
contre ses portes de verre

* * *

I dedicate this poem
to my inability
to understand my immediate
circle

At times like these
that don't take place
that leave me
beyond all comprehension

I dedicate it to the right words
that I can never utter
to denounce this barbarous
and shameless century

* * *

My father's house
a madhouse
contained the world's vast history
reduced to a few volumes
in a locked-up library

I banged cursing
on its glass doors

* * *

La guerre a éclaté
la télévision
nous livre à domicile
les blessés et les morts du jour
farcis de fromage
et de pâtes

Parfois quelqu'un sort
de table pour cracher
des arêtes inexistantes

* * *

Dans les vitrines des magasins
la vie de tous les jours se mire
avec ses passants
sa circulation

Elle aussi est à vendre
avec ses intrigues
ses drames
sa pourriture cachée

Mon chemin se rétracte –
à l'intérieur de mon corps
je change de direction

* * *

War has broken out
television
delivers to our homes
the day's dead and injured
with a cheese and pasta
stuffing

Sometimes someone leaves
the table to spit out
non-existent fish-bones

* * *

In shop windows
daily life is reflected
with its passers-by
its traffic

It too is for sale
with its intrigues
its dramas
its unseen decay

My path retracts –
inside my body
I change direction

* * *

Courez dit-il
toute la ville est en feu
l'homme brûlait

Où faut-il aller
demandai-je
dans la mer répondit-il

Je flamboyai à mon tour
phosphorescente
avec des yeux comme des phares

* * *

Sur une mappemonde
je provoque le déluge

Les océans fusionnent
les montagnes se noient

Il n'y a pas d'arche

J'étouffe Dieu
avec mes cheveux

* * *

Run he said
the whole town's ablaze
the man was on fire

Where should I go
I asked
into the sea he replied

I blazed in turn
phosphorescent
with headlight-like eyes

* * *

On a map of the world
I bring about the deluge

Oceans merge
mountains drown

There is no ark

I smother God
with my hair

* * *

Dans le fleuve
où je suis née
j'ai noyé mes parents

En signe de deuil
je porte le plumage noir
de ma mère-corbeau

* * *

Même si j'habite un pays
froid et sans lumière
où j'ai grandi parmi fraudeurs et
assassins

Je vis sur les berges du Nil
depuis de millénaires
pétrifiée par le soleil
au bord du fleuve
je n'ose pas dormir

* * *

In the river
where I was born
I drowned my parents

As a mark of mourning
I wear my crow-mother's
black plumage

* * *

Though I live in a cold
and lightless land
where I grew up with swindlers and
assassins

I have lived on the banks of the Nile
for thousands of years
petrified by the sun
at the water's edge
I dare not sleep

* * *

Océan je suis les humeurs
d'une lune en folie
j'accompagne les poissons
dans leurs migrations

Chacune de mes vagues
est une révolte
qui fait chavirer vos bateaux
saccage vos plages

* * *

Mon père m'a transmis son nom
comme un pouvoir magique

Déversant son sang sur ma tête
lors de mon baptême
il ignorait
que les noms se vengent
de celui qui les lègue
et finissent par tuer

* * *

Ocean I follow the moods
of an ecstatic moon
I go with the fish
on their migration

Each of my waves
is a revolt
that capsizes your ships
devastates your beaches

* * *

My father handed me down his name
like a magic power

Pouring his blood onto my head
during my christening
he was unaware
that names punish
he who bequeaths them
and end up killing

* * *

Mon frère plongeur sous-marin
ne sait plus marcher

Flanqué de nageoires tranchantes
il refuse le monde non-aquatique
pollué et corrompu

Il s'allie aux requins
et s'attaque à quiconque
s'introduit
dans ses eaux

SABLE

Tandis que les horloges décapitent
les heures
abrégeant notre temps
le présent tricote
sans relâche le passé
dans des lieux abandonnés

* * *

My deep-sea diving brother
can no longer walk

Flanked by sharp fins
he rejects the polluted and corrupt
non-aquatic world

He sides with the sharks
and attacks anyone
who enters
his waters

SAND

While clocks decapitate
the hours
curtailing our time
the present relentlessly
knits the past
in deserted spots

CIEL

Ma vie est un livre
que je n'ai pas écrit

Je l'accompagne malgré moi
page par page
ignorant
ce que je vis
ce qui m'attend

Je suis le cauchemar d'un Dieu fou

VENT

Le mot change
une fois posé
sur le blanc de la page

La lumière ne l'atteint plus
coupées de leur environnement
les tempêtes tourbillonnent sans lui

Dans le recueil fermé
sa solitude
est sans nom

SKY

My life is a book
that I didn't write

I follow it against my will
page by page
not knowing
what I experience
what awaits me

I am the nightmare of a mad God

WIND

The word changes
once placed
on the whiteness of the page

Light can no longer reach it
cut off from their surroundings
storms swirl without it

In the closed collection
its solitude
has no name

* * *

J'ai peur du livre
qui me regarde
de ses pages blanches
parsemées de signes

Qui sont-ils ?
Déterrés par mes yeux
ils existent
à l'endroit où tout peut naître
mais s'éteignent
dès que les mots plaident
pour les mots

* * *

Dans ce monde
démuni de sens
la langage est notre ultime refuge

C'est lui qui appelle notre présent
à exister

J'appâte le papier
pour qu'il se couche
sous mon écriture

* * *

I'm afraid of the book
that watches me
from its white pages
studded with characters

Who are they?
Disinterred by my eyes
they exist
in the place where everything can be born
but are extinguished
the moment words plead
for words

* * *

In this world
stripped of meaning
language is our last refuge

It is what bids our present
exist

I entice the page
so that it may lie
beneath my writing

* * *

Tu voudrais connaître la source
d'où jaillissent mes poèmes

Il n'y a qu'un cratère
parsemé de cailloux

Un œil d'ange déchu
au regard béant
veille nuit et jour

Celui qui s'approche
est dévoré tout cru

Seuls les cheveux seront recrachés

* * *

Mes poèmes sont des peaux
abandonnées
perdus dans les mots
dévorés par eux

* * *

You would know the spring
from which my poems flow

There is but one crater
studded with pebbles

The eye of a fallen angel
with a cavernous stare
watches night and day

Anyone who approaches
is devoured uncooked

Only the hair will be spat out

* * *

My poems are discarded
skins
lost in the words
devoured by them

* * *

Je me débats
sous l'avalanche des mots

Je vous fais signe
de ne pas approcher

Chaque nuit
les loups me dévorent

CHALEUR

Entends-tu le feuillage
frémir sur mon nom

Je n'habite pas cette ville
mes rêves
loups affamés qui rôdent
sont restés sauvages

Lorsque ma meute
rencontrera la tienne
nous chasserons ensemble

* * *

I struggle
beneath the avalanche of words

I signal
to stop you approaching

Each night
wolves devour me

HEAT

Do you hear the leaves
quiver over my name

I do not reside in this town
my dreams
famished wolves that prowl
have remained wild

When my pack
meets yours
we shall hunt together

FROID

Au bord de la nuit
ma mère est assise
ses vêtements en loques
deux crocs
dans sa bouche édentée

Elle se jette sur moi
et me suce la moelle

ENTRE CHIEN ET LOUP

Une nuit
au-delà de la nuit
nous attend

Une nuit
au-delà de tout savoir

Elle nous efface
de son tableau noir

Nous sommes immortels
tant que nous vivons

COLD

At the edge of night
my mother is seated
her clothes in tatters
two fangs
in her toothless mouth

She throws herself on me
and sucks out my marrow

AT DUSK: BETWEEN DOG AND WOLF

A night
beyond night
awaits us

A night
beyond all knowledge

It wipes us
from its blackboard

We are immortal
as long as we live

from
FIRE-EATER
L'AVALEUR DE FEU

To René
(in memoriam)

I

* * *

Il est parti
sans se retourner

Son ange désorienté
se tient immobile
les ailes tachées
de sang

Mon souffle prononce
le nom de l'aimé
il n'est qu'un peu de buée
quelques lettres
de l'alphabet

Avec mes cheveux
ma tristesse continue
de pousser

I

* * *

He left
without turning round

His angel disorientated
stands still
wings stained
with blood

My breath utters
the beloved's name
it is but a little mist
a few letters
of the alphabet

Along with my hair
my sadness continues
to grow

* * *
à René

Il n'y a pas de route
plus longue
que vers toi

Chaque arrivée
est un mirage

Dans ton silence
écoute ma voix
qui approche

* * *

Tu es celui
avec qui je lutte
sur une couche d'enfer
ange de mes terribles nuits
Tu as fait de moi
un avaleur de feu

* * *
to René

There is no road
longer
than to you

Each arrival
is a mirage

In your silence
listen to my voice
approaching

* * *

You are the one
with whom I struggle
on a bed of hell
angel of my terrible nights
you have made of me
a fire-eater

* * *

Lorsque mon amour est né
je l'ai lavé
de ma main droite

Lorsque mon amour est mort
je l'ai lavé
de ma main gauche

Sans futur
je subsiste
les deux mains coupées

II

* * *

Depuis toujours
je suis assise
devant la page blanche
sans avoir le courage
de la tourner

* * *

When my love was born
I washed him
with my right hand

When my love died
I washed him
with my left hand

Without a future
I stay behind
both hands severed

II

* * *

All my life
I have sat
in front of the blank page
lacking the courage
to turn it

* * *

Ma mémoire est lourde
comme un vaisseau qui coule

J'ai vogué
dans toutes les parties du monde
les dieux m'égorgeaient
je les égorgeais –

Ecrivant dans leurs bouches
dans leurs entrailles
j'ai oublié la poésie –

je suis devenue poète

* * *

La lune a empoisonné mes livres
je ne retrouve plus mes mots
les pages vides
m'observent et me poursuivent
comme des loups

* * *

My memory is heavy
like a sinking ship

I have wandered
all over the world
the gods slit my throat
I slit theirs –

Writing in their mouths
in their entrails
I forgot poetry –

I became a poet

* * *

The moon has poisoned my books
I can no longer find my words
the empty pages
watch me and hound me
like wolves

* * *

Je me décline à toutes les personnes
ma présence est devenue
de plus en plus incertaine

Ma langue transformée
en betterave rouge
végète dans ma bouche

III

* * *

Dans les abattoirs de l'église
on nous transforme
en vautours

Nous dévorons
le corps du Christ
plongeant nos cous
dans son sang
avec une violence inavouée

* * *

I fade for everyone
my presence has become
more and more uncertain

My tongue turned
into a beetroot
vegetates in my mouth

III

* * *

In the abattoirs of the church
we are turned
into vultures

We devour
the body of Christ
plunging our necks
into his blood
with unconfessed violence

* * *

Je cherche un baptistère
pour y rendre mon nom
pour le noyer
dans son eau bénite

Je reprends sur moi
le péché originel
comme une force
une carapace
qui me rend invulnérable

* * *

Aucune de nos complaintes
ne sera entendue

Dieu est sourd-muet
Personne ne nous a appris
le langage gestuel

* * *

I'm searching for a baptistery
to return my name
to drown it
in its holy water

I retrieve
original sin
like a force
a carapace
that makes me invulnerable

* * *

None of our laments
will be heard

God is deaf and dumb
No one has taught us
sign language

* * *

L'ange déchu
qui se mirait
dans l'eau
s'est noyé
dans son image

* * *

Le septième jour
Dieu s'assoupit

La terre tremble toujours
sous ses ronflements

* * *

The fallen angel
who gazed at his reflection
in the water
drowned
in his image

* * *

On the seventh day
God dozed off

The earth is still shaken
by his snoring

IV

* * *

A mon réveil
je ramasse
victimes et débris
de mes rêves
entassés dans un coin
de ma chambre

* * *

Tiré par des chiens
le temps glisse
sur une neige invisible
dans son traîneau de fer

Si tu t'endors
il te traversera

IV

* * *

When I wake up
I collect
the victims and debris
of my dreams
stacked in a corner
of my bedroom

* * *

Drawn by dogs
time glides
over invisible snow
in its iron sleigh

If you fall asleep
it will pass through you

* * *

La nuit
j'entends les morts
qui traversent ma chambre

Recouverts de plumes
tachetés de sang
ils s'abattent sur moi
me fouillant
entre les jambes

Apres le massacre
d'un claquement d'ailes
ils s'envolent

* * *

Maintenant que je suis habituée
à ce corps
faut-il l'abandonner à la terre
le soustraire au soleil

Il ne sera que cendres –
mais je les lancerai
autour de moi
avec fureur

* * *

At night
I hear the dead
crisscross my bedroom

Covered with feathers
speckled with blood
they swoop down on me
fumbling
between my legs

After the massacre
with a flapping of wings
they fly off

* * *

Now I am grown used
to this body
must I surrender it to the earth
hide it from the sun

It will be just ashes –
but I shall fling them
around me
frenziedly

* * *

Je partirai
sans souliers
sans chemin

Désemparé
mon ange gardien
jettera la monture
de ses ailes

* * *

Chaque nuit
je m'entraîne à mourir
j'explore la cartographie
de l'au-delà

Dans les villes où je passe
j'organise des expositions
de mes rêves
et je les vends au marché noir

* * *

I shall leave
shoeless
aimless

Distraught
my guardian angel
will discard the mounting
for his wings

* * *

Every night
I practise dying
I explore the cartography
of the hereafter

In the towns through which I pass
I organise exhibitions
of my dreams
and sell them on the black market

V

* * *

Mon absence
longtemps commencée
avant mon départ
se prolonge
au-delà de mon retour

* * *

Après le passage
des prophètes
l'herbe a reverdi

Ils sont partis
portant le fardeau
de leurs paroles sur le dos

Tenant en laisse
leur dieu tout-puissant

V

* * *

My absence
begun long ago
before my departure
stretches
beyond my return

* * *

After the passing
of the prophets
the grass is green again

They left
carrying the burden
of their words on their backs

Holding on a leash
their all-powerful god

* * *

Combien de fois
ai-je tourné
autour le soleil

Même en dormant
je continue
à accompagner la terre
blottie sous mes couvertures
comme un animal
qui hiverne

VI

* * *

A ma naissance
ma mère a fait de moi
de nombreuses copies
aucune ne me ressemblait

Déjà elle me cherchait
parmi les morts

* * *

How many times
have I revolved
around the sun

Even asleep
I continue
to follow the earth
huddled under my blankets
like a wintering
animal

VI

* * *

At my birth
my mother made
many copies of me
none of which resembled me

Already she searched for me
among the dead

* * *

L'enfant dévore la lune de miel
de ses parents

Il brise la table des lois
sur leur dos

Et les moissonne comme un champ

* * *

Je suis l'erreur fatale
de mon père

Le vent du nord hurle
dans ma bouche
j'annonce le gel

* * *

The child devours his parents'
honeymoon

He smashes the table of the laws
on their backs

And reaps them like a field

* * *

I am my father's
fatal error

The north wind howls
in my mouth
I herald the frost

* * *

Il ne faut pas chercher
le père dans le père
ni la mère
dans la mère

ils m'ont inventée
en me sculptant
à coups de hache

* * *

Do not seek
the father in the father
nor the mother
in the mother

they invented me
sculpting me
with an axe

from
BLESSED BE THE SERPENT
BÉNI SOIT LE SERPENT

I

* * *

Ne me retiens pas
je vais disparaître
comme une anguille
dans les profondeurs
de l'eau

Déjà je respire
à travers des branchies

La lune mon alliée
ricoche dans l'eau
pour brouiller ma piste

I

* * *

Don't hold me back
I'm going to disappear
like an eel
into the depths
of the water

Already I'm breathing
through gills

The moon my ally
ricochets in the water
to cover my tracks

* * *

Ma mère
m'habille de brouillard
et m'épuise

Sans cesse
elle me fait ressusciter
d'une poignée de terre
où elle a planté sa croix

Je suis son ascenseur arrêté
entre deux paysages

* * *

J'ai eu des centaines de mères
jeunes ou âgées
avec ou sans béquilles

Toutes ont refusé de m'allaiter
affamée à côté d'elles
je croupissais
enfonçant mes racines
dans la terre
pour me nourrir

* * *

My mother
dresses me in fog
and exhausts me

Ceaselessly
she resuscitates me
from a handful of earth
in which she has planted her cross

I am her lift stuck
between two landscapes

* * *

I had hundreds of mothers
young and old
with and without crutches

All refused to suckle me
starving at their sides
I grew weaker
burying my roots
in the earth
to nourish myself

* * *

Mes pieds sans racines
vagabondent sur terre
en quête d'un horizon habitable
où je laisserai tomber ma peau
pour savoir si j'existe

* * *

Etranger je demeure –

La terre émigre
sous mes pas

Marchant sur des couteaux
je cherche une patrie
dans ton sang

* * *

My rootless feet
roam the earth
in search of a habitable horizon
where I shall drop my skin
to know if I exist

* * *

Foreigner I remain –

The earth emigrates
beneath my feet

Walking on knives
I seek a homeland
in your blood

* * *

Sous ma peau
un métro
fait vibrer
mes fondations

Des stations s'inventent
dans la circulation
de mon sang

Sur les perrons
revenus du passé
des voyageurs attendent

Ma tête terminus
sera leur fosse commune

* * *

Under my skin
a metro
shakes
my foundations

Stations are invented
in the circulation
of my blood

On flights of steps
returned from the past
travellers wait

My terminus head
will be their common grave

* * *

Sur le corps de ma mère
étaient inscrites
ma date de naissance
celle de ma disparition

Pierre tombale ambulante
je la portais
sur mon épaule

Sous ce fardeau invisible
je me suis écroulée

* * *

Où que j'aille
j'emporte mon cadavre
avec moi

Chaque soir
je l'immole
au soleil couchant

Ensemble nous badigeonnons le ciel
de sang

* * *

On my mother's body
were inscribed
my date of birth
that of my disappearance

Itinerant gravestone
I carried her
on my shoulders

Beneath this invisible burden
I collapsed

* * *

Wherever I go
I carry my corpse
with me

Each night
I sacrifice it
to the setting sun

Together we daub the sky
with blood

II

IL SATIRO DANZANTE
pour Elio Pecora

Resurgi des tréfonds de l'océan
le satire amputé
danse et virevolte

Jetant la gravité
se hissant sur les cimes de l'espace
il danse

A travers ses pas d'évasion
il épuise sa folie
et fatigue l'infini

II

IL SATIRO DANZANTE
for Elio Pecora

Risen from the depths of the ocean
the amputated satyr
dances and twirls

Discarding gravity
heaving himself up onto the crests of space
he dances

Through his evasive steps
he exhausts his madness
and wearies infinity

* * *

Pendant la nuit
je hurle comme un loup

Mon dos est recouvert
d'un épais pelage
je rôde près des bergeries

A mon réveil
je consulte le miroir
pour découvrir une Anise Koltz familière
au regard innocent –

Mais avec des babines recouvertes de sang frais

III

* * *

La lune vient se reposer
sous mon édredon

Elle compte une à une
mes vertèbres
pour s'endormir

Tandis que la terre
continue à tituber
dans l'espace

* * *

During the night
I howl like a wolf

My back is covered
with a thick coat
I prowl around sheep barns

When I wake
I look in the mirror
and see a familiar Anise Koltz
with an innocent air –

But with my chops covered in fresh blood

III

* * *

The moon comes and settles
under my eiderdown

She counts one by one
my vertebrae
to get to sleep

While the earth
continues to stagger
in space

* * *

L'immensité de la mer
me traverse

Elle déborde
de mes souliers

* * *

Le soleil tend des filets
aux oiseaux
et les dévore au soir
crachant leurs ombres

* * *

The vastness of the sea
passes through me

It overflows
from my shoes

* * *

The sun sets a trap
for the birds
and devours them in the evening
spitting out their shadows

IV

* * *

Mes mots sont habitués à la guerre
aux bombardements atomiques
aux camps de concentration

Mes mots sous-alimentés
anémiques
ont des yeux pleins d'effroi

* * *

Il n'y a pas d'espoir
dans le poème
ni de certitude

Je vous enterre
dans les tombes béantes
qui apparaissent
entre les mots
puis devant chaque question
je m'effondre

IV

* * *

My words are grown used to war
to atom-bomb attacks
to concentration camps

My malnourished anaemic
words
have terror-filled eyes

* * *

There is no hope
in the poem
nor certainty

I bury you
in the cavernous tombs
that appear
between words
then facing each question
I collapse

* * *

La vie dépend
de chaque mot

Je laisserai en friche
un monde de non-dit
si je me tais

* * *

Par l'écriture
je pénètre
dans l'impossible

Sous les écorchures des lettres
l'encre qui coule est mon sang

* * *

Life depends
on each word

I shall leave uncultivated
a world of unsaid
if I remain silent

* * *

Through writing
I penetrate
the impossible

Beneath the grazes of the letters
the ink that flows is my blood

* * *

L'écriture
est dans l'impossible
avec elle
je visite l'enfer

* * *

Mon poème
est un pain brûlant

Mangez-le
il est mon corps

Il invente futur
et passé
pour échapper au présent

* * *

Writing
is in the impossible
with it
I visit hell

* * *

My poem
is hot bread

Eat it
it is my body

It invents future
and past
in order to escape the present

* * *

Lorsque les paroles
n'habiteront plus
ma bouche

Je la comblerai
de pierres

V

* * *

Depuis 76 ans
je suis immortelle

Je m'élève dans le ciel
sur mon balai de sorcière
être humain terne et gris –
je ressemble de loin
à un énorme busard

Je répète mon nom
comme un mantra
de crainte de l'oublier

* * *

When words
no longer inhabit
my mouth

I shall fill it
with stones

V

* * *

For 76 years
I have been immortal

I rise into the sky
on my witch's broom
human being drab and grey –
I look from a distance
like a huge harrier

I repeat my name
like a mantra
for fear of forgetting it

* * *

Je déracine des étoiles
et sur les têtes des passants
je les jette

Ils se courbent de douleur –
les chiens commencent à hurler
on annonce la pluie

VI

* * *

à René Koltz

Tes pas ont inventé
mon parcours

Comme un chien
je suis tes traces
léchant mes blessures

* * *

I uproot stars
and onto the heads of passers-by
I throw them

They double-up in pain –
dogs start howling
rain is forecast

VI

* * *

to René Koltz

Your steps invented
my path

Like a dog
I follow your tracks
licking my wounds

* * *

Nous parlons des langues différentes –
tu m'enseignes des mots d'amour
que j'apprends par cœur

Pendant que j'hiberne seule
ils blanchissent mes cheveux

VII

* * *

Béni soit le serpent
qui m'apprit la désobéissance

Ma tête était une filiale de banque
un office de travail

Je me purifie
je ne prie plus

J'allume le feu de mon enfer
et je chante

* * *

We speak different languages –
you teach me words of love
that I learn off by heart

While I hibernate alone
they whiten my hair

VII

* * *

Blessed be the serpent
who taught me disobedience

My head was a banking subsidiary
an employment agency

I purify myself
I no longer pray

I light the fires of my hell
and I sing

* * *

Apres avoir verrouillé
le paradis
Dieu partit sur une chamelle
avec la terre
sous le bras

* * *

Having bolted up
paradise
God set out on a she-camel
the earth
tucked under His arm

BIOGRAPHICAL NOTES

ANISE KOLTZ was born in Luxembourg in 1928. She is first and foremost a poet, but is also a translator and photographer. She has written poetry in German and French, and also children's books in Luxembourgish.

In 1963 she founded and directed the Journées littéraires de Mondorf (Mondorf Literary Days), which brought together writers from all over the world, with the aim of establishing and maintaining links between the Luxembourg and the international literary scene. She continued in this role until 1974. In 1995, the Mondorf Literary Days were revived and it was decided that all genres would be represented, thereby providing a wide range of authors with a platform for their works.

Koltz is a member of the Académie Mallarmé (Paris), Pen-Club Belgium and the Institut Grand-Ducal des Arts et des Lettres (Luxembourg). She is one of the founding members and vice-president of The European Academy of Poetry. Over the years she has collaborated with, and translated, poets, writers and artists to create bibliophilic editions, has had a variety of works dedicated to her and has had poems set to music.

Translations of her poetry have appeared in Belgium, Colombia, Germany, Ireland, Italy, Macedonia, Portugal, Romania, Spain and Sweden; she has received many prizes and awards for her poetry.

ANNE-MARIE GLASHEEN, poet, photographer and translator, with an English mother and Belgian father, spent her early childhood in Belgium. A past Chair of the Translators Association, Glasheen has translated fiction, non-fiction, plays, poetry and art history books. Her translated plays have been performed at the Edinburgh and Brighton festivals, in London, the USA and Northern Ireland. In 1998, she was the recipient of the Belgian francophone prize for translation. She co-ordinates cultural exchange programmes and festivals, runs literary projects, gives public readings, lectures and broadcasts, runs workshops and writes articles.

Her poetry has been published in poetry journals in Belgium, France, Ireland, Luxembourg, the UK and USA and her first collection appeared with Bradshaw Books in 2008. As a photographer her work has been widely exhibited in and around London. Her first major show outside the UK was in Cork, Ireland, in October 2008.

CAROLINE PRICE was born in 1956 in Middlesex. She studied Music at York University and violin at the Guildhall School of Music and Drama in London, and has worked as a violinist and teacher in Glasgow, London and Kent, where she now lives.

She has published three collections of poetry, the latest of which, *Wishbone*, appeared with Shoestring Press in 2008. Her poems have won many awards and been published in a wide range of magazines and anthologies over the past twenty years. She has written reviews, has undertaken commissions for Kent and Medway Councils, and has co-edited *Four Caves of the Heart*, (Headland, 2004), an anthology of women's poetry.

In 1997 she was one of ten women poets from Kent, Ireland, France, Francophone Belgium and Flanders who participated in the MUZE tour, discussing and reading their work in Kent and Northern Europe. She is a founder member of the N7 poetry workshop in north London, and an active supporter of the Kent & Sussex Poetry Society.

Also available in the Arc Publications
'VISIBLE POETS' SERIES
(Series Editor: Jean Boase-Beier)

No. 1
MIKLÓS RADNÓTI (Hungary)
Camp Notebook
TRANSLATED BY FRANCIS JONES
INTRODUCED BY GEORGE SZIRTES

No. 2
BARTOLO CATTAFI (Italy)
Anthracite
TRANSLATED BY BRIAN COLE
INTRODUCED BY PETER DALE
(Poetry Book Society Recommended Translation)

No. 3
MICHAEL STRUNGE (Denmark)
A Virgin from a Chilly Decade
TRANSLATED BY BENTE ELSWORTH
INTRODUCED BY JOHN FLETCHER

No. 4
TADEUSZ RÓZEWICZ (Poland)
recycling
TRANSLATED BY BARBARA BOGOCZEK (PLEBANEK) & TONY HOWARD
INTRODUCED BY ADAM CZERNIAWSKI

No. 5
CLAUDE DE BURINE (France)
Words Have Frozen Over
TRANSLATED BY MARTIN SORRELL
INTRODUCED BY SUSAN WICKS

No. 6
CEVAT ÇAPAN (Turkey)
Where Are You, Susie Petschek?
TRANSLATED BY CEVAT ÇAPAN & MICHAEL HULSE
INTRODUCED BY A. S. BYATT

No.7
JEAN CASSOU (France)
33 Sonnets of the Resistance
WITH AN ORIGINAL INTRODUCTION BY LOUIS ARAGON
TRANSLATED BY TIMOTHY ADÈS
INTRODUCED BY ALISTAIR ELLIOT

No. 8
ARJEN DUINKER (Holland)
The Sublime Song of a Maybe
TRANSLATED BY WILLEM GROENEWEGEN
INTRODUCED BY JEFFREY WAINWRIGHT

No. 9
MILA HAUGOVÁ (Slovakia)
Scent of the Unseen
TRANSLATED BY JAMES & VIERA SUTHERLAND-SMITH
INTRODUCED BY FIONA SAMPSON

No. 10
ERNST MEISTER (Germany)
Between Nothing and Nothing
TRANSLATED BY JEAN BOASE-BEIER
INTRODUCED BY JOHN HARTLEY WILLIAMS

No. 11
YANNIS KONDOS (Greece)
Absurd Athlete
TRANSLATED BY DAVID CONNOLLY
INTRODUCED BY DAVID CONSTANTINE

No. 12
BEJAN MATUR (Turkey)
In the Temple of a Patient God
TRANSLATED BY RUTH CHRISTIE
INTRODUCED BY MAUREEN FREELY

No. 13
GABRIEL FERRATER (Catalonia / Spain)
Women and Days
TRANSLATED BY ARTHUR TERRY
INTRODUCED BY SEAMUS HEANEY

No. 14
INNA LISNIANSKAYA (Russia)
Far from Sodom
TRANSLATED BY DANIEL WEISSBORT
INTRODUCED BY ELAINE FEINSTEIN

No. 15
SABINE LANGE (Germany)
The Fishermen Sleep
Translated by Jenny Williams
Introduced by Mary O'Donnell

No. 16
TAKAHASHI MUTSUO (Japan)
We of Zipangu
Translated by James Kirkup & Tamaki Makoto
Introduced by Glyn Pursglove

No. 17
JURIS KRONBERGS (Latvia)
Wolf One-Eye
Translated by Mara Rozitis
Introduced by Jaan Kaplinski

No. 18
REMCO CAMPERT (Holland)
I Dreamed in the Cities at Night
Translated by Donald Gardner
Introduced by Paul Vincent

No. 19
DOROTHEA ROSA HERLIANY (Indonesia)
Kill the Radio
Translated by Harry Aveling
Introduced by Linda France

No. 20
SOLEÏMAN ADEL GUÉMAR (Algeria)
State of Emergency
Translated by Tom Cheesman & John Goodby
Introduced by Lisa Appignanesi

No. 21
ELI TOLARETXIPI (Spain / Basque)
Still Life with Loops
Translated by Philip Jenkins
Introduced by Robert Crawford

No. 22
FERNANDO KOFMAN (Argentina)
The Flights of Zarza
TRANSLATED BY IAN TAYLOR
INTRODUCED BY ANDREW GRAHAM-YOOLL

No. 23
LARISSA MILLER (Russia)
Guests of Eternity
TRANSLATED BY RICHARD MCKANE
INTRODUCED BY SASHA DUGDALE